SPACE JOKES

Compiled by Pam Rosenberg
Illustrated by Patrick Girouard

The Child's World

Special thanks to Donna Hynek and her second grade class of 2005–2006 for sharing their favorite jokes.

Published in the United States of America by The Child's World®
PO Box 326, Chanhassen, MN 55317-0326
800-599-READ
www.childsworld.com

Acknowledgments
   The Child's World®: Mary Berendes, Publishing Director

   Editorial Directions, Inc.: E. Russell Primm, Editorial Director and Line Editor; Katie Marsico, Managing Editor; Assistant Editor, Caroline Wood; Susan Ashley, Proofreader

   The Design Lab: Kathleen Petelinsek, Designer; Kari Tobin, Page Production

Library of Congress Cataloging-in-Publication Data
   Space jokes / compiled by Pam Rosenberg; illustrated by Patrick Girouard.
      p. cm. — (Laughing matters)
   ISBN-13 978-1-59296-710-0
   ISBN-10 1-59296-710-8 (library bound : alk. paper)
   1. Outer space—Juvenile humor. 2. Space flight—Juvenile humor.
   I. Rosenberg, Pam. II. Girouard, Patrick. III. Title. IV. Series.
   PN6231.S645S63 2007
   818'.602080356—dc22   2006022656

ASTRONAUTS

If athletes get athlete's foot, what do astronauts get?
Missile toe.

When do astronauts have lunch?
At launch time.

Astronaut: Wanna fly?
Copilot: Sure
Astronaut: Wait a second—I'll catch one for you!

What do you call a crazy astronaut?
An astro-nut.

What state has the most astronauts?
Moon-tana.

What kind of music do astronauts like?
Nep-tunes.

What did the astronaut serve drinks in?
Sunglasses.

How does an astronaut keep up her pants?
With an asteroid belt.

What kind of plates do astronauts like to eat off of?
Flying saucers.

What do astronauts shave with?
Laser razors.

First Astronaut: I'm hungry!
Second Astronaut: So am I. It must be launch time!

What did the astronaut cook for lunch?
An unidentified frying object.

What's an astronaut's favorite fish?
Starfish.

How do you put a baby astronaut to sleep?
You rock-et.

What's an astronaut's favorite place on the computer?
The space bar.

Where do astronauts park their spaceships?
At parking meteors.

Why did the astronaut buy a bulletproof vest?
To protect herself from shooting stars.

What do astronauts do when they get dirty?
They take a meteor shower.

Why did the lazy student think he could be an astronaut?
His teacher told him he was taking up space.

What do you call an astronaut who is afraid of heights?
A failure.

Why did the astronaut bang her head against the wall?
She wanted to see stars.

Which astronaut goes into space the most?
Sir Launch-a lot.

Why did the astronaut take a shovel into space? To dig a black hole.

Two astronauts were in a spacecraft circling thousands of miles above Earth. The plan was for one astronaut to leave the ship and go on a fifteen-minute space walk. The other astronaut was to stay inside the spacecraft.

After completing his walk, the first astronaut tried to get back inside the spacecraft, but the door was locked. He knocked, but there was no answer. He knocked again. Still no answer. Then he pounded as hard as he could.

Finally, after what seemed like hours, he heard a voice from inside the spacecraft: "Who's there?"

9

Dan: I know a planet you can see both day and night.
Nick: Really? Which one?
Dan: Earth.

Why did Mickey Mouse go to space?
To find Pluto.

When is the moon the heaviest?
When it is full.

Why is the moon like a dollar?
Because it has four quarters.

How is a telephone like the planet Saturn?
They both have rings.

Why wouldn't you want to give Saturn a bath?
Because it would leave a ring around your tub.

What do moon people do after their weddings?
They go on a honeyearth.

What is soft, white, and comes from Mars? Martian-mallows.

What holds the moon up? Moon beams.

Student: Sir, did you hear that scientists have found life on another planet?
Teacher: What are you talking about?
Student: They found fleas on Pluto!

Which is heavier—a full moon or a half moon? A half moon. The full moon is lighter.

What travels around Earth all year but doesn't use a drop of fuel? The moon.

What was the name of the first satellite to orbit Earth? The moon!

What does the sun do when it gets tired? It sets a while.

Why is the sun the smartest star?
Because it's so bright.

14

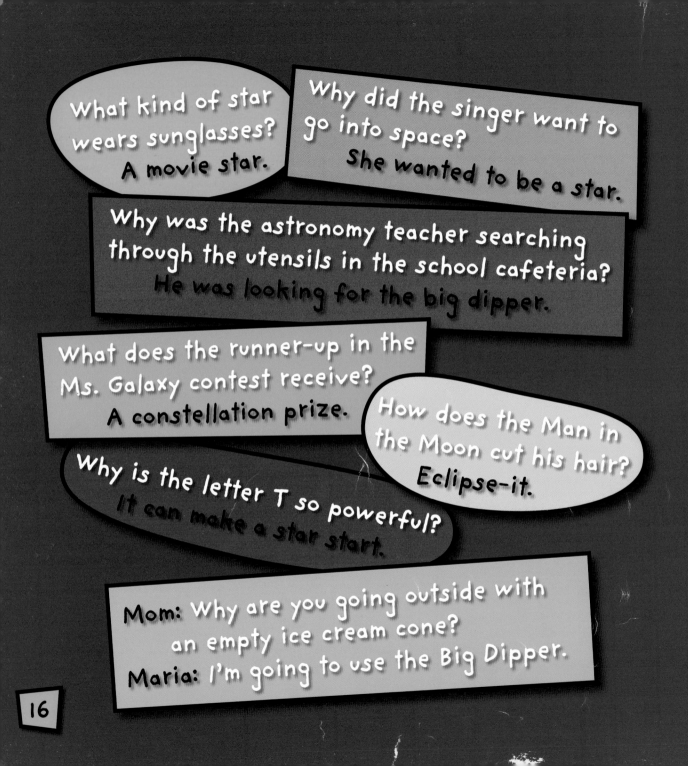

THE MARTIANS ARE COMING!

What would you get if you crossed a 50-foot-tall Martian with a 300-pound chicken?
The biggest cluck in the universe.

What's the most popular snack on Mars?
Marsmallows.

Where do Martians go fishing?
In the galax-seas.

What do Martians do when they get thirsty?
They take a drink from the Big Dipper.

What is normal eyesight for a Martian?
20 – 20 – 20

Why can't a Martian's nose be 12 inches long?
If it were, it would be a foot!

Pete: What's the difference between a Martian and snoo?
Russell: What's snoo?
Pete: Nothing much. What's snoo with you?

17

ANIMALS IN SPACE

What kind of saddle do you put on a space horse?
A saddle-lite.

What would you get if you crossed a galaxy and a toad?
Star Warts.

Where do cow astronauts travel?
To the moooooooon.

What do you get when you cross a comet with a guppy?
A starfish.

What do space squirrels like to eat?
Astro-nuts.

THE REST OF THE UNIVERSE

What kind of poem can you find in space?
Uni-verse.

What do you call a space magician?
A flying sorcerer.

What goes up when you count down?
A rocket.

What's a space creature's favorite food?
Human beans.

What kind of years weigh the least?
Light years.

About Patrick Girouard:

Patrick Girouard has been illustrating books for almost 15 years but still looks remarkably lifelike. He loves reading, movies, coffee, robots, a beautiful red-haired lady named Rita, and especially his sons, Marc and Max. Here's an interesting fact: A dog named Sam lives under his drawing board. You can visit him (Patrick, not Sam) at www.pgirouard.com.

About Pam Rosenberg:

Pam Rosenberg is a former junior high school teacher and corporate trainer. She currently works as an author, editor, and the mother of Sarah and Jake. She took on this project as a service to all her fellow parents of young children. At least now their kids will have lots of jokes to choose from when looking for the one they will tell their parents over and over and over again!